(((sound advice on)))
COMPRESSORS, LIMITERS, EXPANDERS, AND GATES

by bill gibson

COURSE TECHNOLOGY
CENGAGE Learning

Australia • Brazil • Japan • Korea • Mexico • Singapore • Spain • United Kingdom • United States

COURSE TECHNOLOGY
CENGAGE Learning·

Sound Advice on Compressors, Limiters, Expanders, and Gates

Bill Gibson

For product information and technology assistance, contact us at **Cengage Learning Customer & Sales Support, 1-800-354-9706**

For permission to use material from this text or product, submit all requests online at **cengage.com/permissions** Further permissions questions can be emailed to **permissionrequest@cengage.com**

ISBN-13: 978-1-931140-24-9
ISBN-10: 1-931140-24-3

Course Technology
25 Thomson Place
Boston, MA 02210
USA

Cengage Learning is a leading provider of customized learning solutions with office locations around the globe, including Singapore, the United Kingdom, Australia, Mexico, Brazil, and Japan. Locate your local office at: **international.cengage.com/region**

Cengage Learning products are represented in Canada by Nelson Education, Ltd.

For your lifelong learning solutions, visit **courseptr.com**
Visit our corporate website at **cengage.com**

Printed in the United States of America
3 4 5 6 7 8 11 10 09 08

Contents

Sound Advice on Compressors, Limiters, Expanders and Gates

Have you noticed that a truly professional recording sounds smooth and blended? That characteristic is, at first, hard to pinpoint and difficult to imitate. Compressors and limiters are often the primary factors in the creation of a commercial sounding mix. A solid understanding of these valuable tools is fundamental in your ability to create impressive and competitive mixes.

How Do They Work?

Compressors and limiters are nothing more than automatic volume controls. When you listen to a guitar solo and the level becomes too loud, it hurts your ears, motivating you to turn the volume down. In the same manner, when the compressor receives an abundance of signal level, it triggers an automatic level control to decrease the signal strength, resulting in a decrease in volume. When the amplitude (signal strength) reaches a certain level (voltage), it surpasses a user-set threshold. As signal exceeds this threshold, an amplifier turns the signal level down according to the compressor/limiter settings. When the signal decreases to below the threshold, the amplifying circuit returns to its original status.

The voltage-controlled amplifier (VCA) circuitry, in the analog domain, is triggered by increases in voltage to turn the signal level down—the amplitude of the waveform is seen by the amplifier as voltage. When the voltage level exceeds the threshold, the signal level is decreased according to the processor settings.

Amplifying circuitry can also be triggered by changes in digital level. These systems are called digitally-controlled amplifiers (DCA). Optically-controlled amplifiers simply alter the signal level in response to audio-induced changes in light intensity. In the purely-digital domain, compression

Sound Advice on Dynamic Processors

settings determine the mathematical calculations that produce audio dynamics.

The VCA, DCA, Optical, and Digital Dynamic Process

VCA (Voltage-Controlled Amplifier)—*An analog amplifier which is controlled by variations in voltage. This is the primary dynamic control circuit in most compressors, limiters, gates, and expanders.*

DCA (Digitally-Controlled Amplifier)—*An analog amplifier which is controlled by variations in digital data. Some of the most highly-regarded consoles combine the warmth and purity of analog circuitry with the precision and flexibility of digital control flexibilties. In addition to precision, digital control data is easily stored, automated, and recalled.*

Optical Level Control—*A very smooth and precise level control system utilizing a light dependent resistor called an opto-isolator. When light shines on this special resistor some of the signal is shunted to ground which reduces the level. Processor parameters are dependent on reactions to light intensity.*

Data Control—*In the digital domain, dynamic control is achieved through mathematical calculations. The actions of the VCA or DCA are simulated according the digitally encoded instructions. As long as the algorithms are well-founded, digital manipulation is very accurate and efficient.*

How Does the Compressor Know What to Compress?

Any amplitude above the user-set threshold will be sensed by the amplifier circuitry and adjusted according to the compressor/limiter settings. Everything above the threshold will be affected by the amplifier circuit; everything below the threshold will remain unchanged.

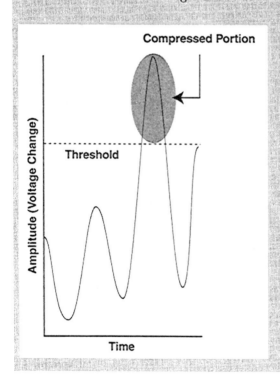

Compressor/limiters, also called dynamic processors, provide a very important function in commercial popular music. As they restrain the loudest sounds, the entire track can be increased in volume, level, or amplitude without overloading circuits, oversaturating the recording media, or harming speakers or ears. The result is not only a more controlled volume, but also a more perceivable, audible, and understandable recording during both the louder and softer passages. Since they're also boosted, quieter sounds become easier to hear and understand, especially when combined with other audio ingredients.

A compressor and limiter both operate on the same principle. The only difference between these dynamic processors is the degree to which they affect the signal that exceeds the threshold. Whereas, a compressor functions as a gentle volume control—which, normally, should be transparent and seamless to the audio process—a limiter is more extreme, radically decreasing the level of the signal that passes above the threshold. Each of these tools has a distinct and important purpose for the creation of professional sounding audio. Often, a very amateur sounding mix is only lacking the punch and aggressive feel that can be created by the proper use of compressors and limiters.

Since the signal that goes though a compressor is passing through an amplifier circuit, this tool must be used carefully to avoid undue introduction of distortion or noise to the signal. Typically, the compressor/limiter should be affecting only the signal with the greatest amplitude, ignoring the bulk of the signal, which does not exceed the threshold. When used this way, a high-quality compressor/limiter is transparent throughout the majority of the audio material, while performing important level control during peak amplitude sections.

Compressor

The goal of the compressor is to gently ride the signal level in the same way that a human engineer would ride the fader while listening to the track playback. In most cases, the listener shouldn't even realize there's a processor being used.

Technical Effect

Technically speaking, a compressor allows the engineer to record an entire track at a hotter level than if the compressor were not included. If the compressor decreases the level of the hottest part of the track by a 6 dB, the entire track can be recorded 6 dB hotter—making up the reduced gain—without over modulating, saturating the tape, or exceeding the maximum digital recording level. Since the compressor should be transparent and seamless as it controls the maximum output level, the result is a more visible, audible, and apparent audio track, especially during the passages containing the least amplitude. In

The Net Result of Compression/Limiting

The true benefit of dynamic control is achieved when a signal is boosted to regain maximum signal level. The low-level signals become much more audible, understandable, and apparent once the reduced gain is made up.

Illustration A represents an audio signal which exceeds the user-set threshold by 6 dB. Utilizing a 6:1 ratio results in a 5 dB gain reduction as the VCA reduces the gain above the threshold—where there was a 6 dB peak, above the threshold, there's now a 1 dB peak (Illustration B). Illustration C represents the result of increasing the overall gain to make up the gain reduction caused by the action of the VCA.

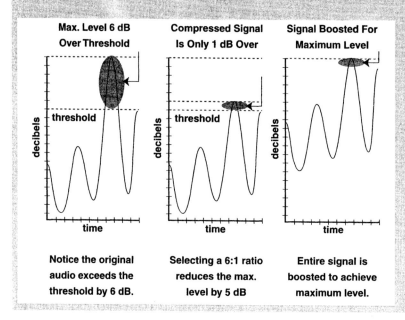

Max. Level 6 dB Over Threshold	Compressed Signal Is Only 1 dB Over	Signal Boosted For Maximum Level
Notice the original audio exceeds the threshold by 6 dB.	Selecting a 6:1 ratio reduces the max. level by 5 dB	Entire signal is boosted to achieve maximum level.

other words, the loud passages should exhibit minimal sonic effect, while the soft passages should be louder than they'd have been without the compressor. Though the compressor/limiter actually controls the loudest passages, the net result for the listener is an increase in the level of the softer passages.

Audio Example 1

Vocal Compressed By 6 dB

Listen to this example of a vocal phrase: first, the original non-compressed recording, then the same phrase compressed by 6 dB.

Musical Effect

Musically speaking, the compressor is very useful. The lead vocal track, for example, should be audible, understandable, and apparent throughout most popular commercial songs; this is precisely the result of compression. A compressed lead vocal track typically sounds more up front in the mix; it remains within its intended dynamic range.

Bass guitar is nearly always compressed. The low-frequency range of the bass contains an abundance of energy; therefore, it produces an abundance of amplitude. Left unchecked, this abundance of low-frequency energy can dominate the overall mix level. For example, when the bass part is particularly strong the overall mix level might be artificially hot. When the bass is properly compressed, however, that energy is kept in check, the bass remains consistently supportive of the mix, and the mix level can be increased.

Any instrument with a wide dynamic range can benefit from compression. However, certain classical and orchestral recordists use little or no compression. The natural dynamic range of the orchestra, piano, symphony, or instrumentalist adds emotional impact and reality to the recording. Many of these recordings are listened to in an environment conducive to such dynamic range: a living room, family room, media room, or listening space designed specifically for the enjoyment of music. In these instances, the natural dynamic range can be appreciated. On the other hand, many commercial popular recordings are listened to in a car, grocery store, mall, or other high ambient noise environments. Any dynamic subtleties might be lost when listened to in these places, so it's important that all the mix ingredients reside within the audible audio spectrum. Therefore, compression is very appropriate for these recordings.

Limiter

A limiter and compressor perform the same basic task, although a compressor controls level and amplitude in a soft and gentle manner, while a limiter controls level and amplitude in an extreme way. The choice to use compression or limiting is purely a musical one. For example, when recording a bass guitarist with a very consistent playing style, there might be little need for compression. However, if the same bassist slaps or snaps during a particular take, a limiter could help level out the amplitude peaks caused by these aggressive musical instances.

Limiters are often used to control the level of an entire mix. An excellent mix typically contains several transient peaks (levels that exceed the average level of the entire mix). Although the limiter ignores the majority of the program material (audio that doesn't exceed the threshold), a peak which exceeds the threshold will be turned down quickly. Through the use of limiters, most commercial recordings maintain a constant and aggressive level and amplitude. A master mix might peak at 0 VU; while the limited mix also peaks at 0 VU, the only difference is that the limited mix sounds louder—a lot louder. A good limiter operates in a way that is imperceptible to most listeners. It reacts quickly to transient peaks and maintains a full, impressive, aggressive sound throughout the limiting process.

Sound Advice on Dynamic Processors

This audio example demonstrates the limiting of a complete mix. On your limiter, the input meter will physically show the level of the non-limited audio before processing. The output meter shows the same audio limited by 6 dB.

Audio Example 2
Making Up Gain That's Been Reduced

Now listen to the difference in volume between the two mixes, once the limited mix is boosted 6 dB to make up the gain reduction.

Controls

Threshold

The threshold setting determines what part of the waveform amplitude the compressor or limiter affects. Any amplitude that exceeds the user-set threshold is turned down in direct proportion to the ratio selected.

Ratio

The ratio setting defines the degree of compression or limiting applied. If the audio signal exceeds the user-set threshold by 7 dB, and the ratio is set at 7:1, the resulting signal exceeds the threshold by only 1 dB. Similarly, if the audio signal exceeds the user-set threshold by 15 dB, and the ratio is set to 5:1 the resulting signal exceeds the threshold by only 3 dB.

Controls on the Compressor/Limiter

Almost all compressor/limiters contain the same control options. Once you understand the functions on one compressor/limiter, you'll find seamless transition to another. The unit pictured here contains the basic controls: attack time, release time, threshold, ratio, output level, peak/RMS, knee, and meter function.

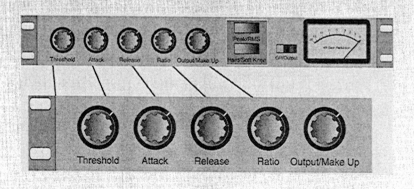

For every 5 dB that the signal exceeds the threshold only 1 dB is allowed—a ratio of 5:1.

The difference between a compressor and a limiter lies in the ratio setting. Ratios of 10:1 and below result in compression; Ratios of more than 10:1 result in limiting. A compressor and limiter are usually within the same piece of equipment. The setting of the ratio control alone determines the function. However, dedicated compressors and limiters are also available. Some compressor/limiters include ratios settings of up to infinity:1. When the ratio is set at infinity:1, the processor simply doesn't allow the level to surpass the user-set threshold by more than 1 dB. Some compressor/limiters include ratio settings of up to only 40:1, or so. This still provides for extreme limiting.

Using the Attack Time Setting to Control Understandability and Punch

The Attack setting provides a means to adjust the relative level of the initial portion of an audio source. In a vocal passage, the initial transient sounds—especially the sounds "s," "t," and "k"—offer two possible complications for recording:

1. *If the vocalist has a natural abundance of transient, the recorded track might take on a harsh character. These transient sounds, called sibilance, can cause distortion of analog tape, irritating effects when reverberated, and they can even overdrive electronic circuitry. In this case, a fast attack time, during compression, helps smooth out the sound—the track will settle into the mix better.*

2. *If the instrumental bed is very percussive, and if the vocal sound contains understated sibilance, the lyrics might be lost in the mix because they're not understandable. In this case, try compressing the vocal track, using a slower attack time; the compressor will let the sibilance pass through unaltered, yet the rest of the word will be compressed according to the control settings. The length of attack time varies with each vocal sound and application, but settings between 5 and 50 ms typically work well. Listen to the sound as you make the attack time adjustment; once you find the right setting, the vocal will seem more alive and understandable.*

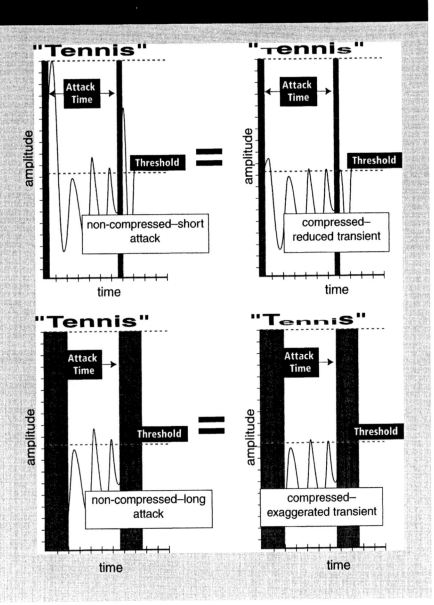

Attack

The attack setting determines how quickly the amplifying circuit (VCA, DCA, or optical) reacts to the incoming signal. There are many musical and technical reasons to select a fast or slow attack time. A vocal, recorded very closely with a sensitive condenser microphone, might contain a lot of transient information (sounds with very fast initial amplitude). The sounds produced by the letters "t," "s," and "k" produce strong and fast attack amplitudes, called transients. When words containing these sounds are recorded using compression or limiting, the transients might be over-exaggerated. If the attack time is set to react too slowly, these transients pass through unaffected while the body of the word, sentence, or phrase is compressed. The result is an artificially intense transient.

Many compressor/limiters provide an attack time range from approximately 0.1 milliseconds to 2.5 seconds—a range of

Hard Knee versus Soft Knee Compression/Limiting

Once the compressor senses signal above the threshold and the attack time has passed, the level-control circuitry begins to respond. A hard knee setting activates the dynamic process immediately; a soft knee setting gradually engages dynamic control during the first 5 dB, or so. Typically, soft knee compression is more gentle and less audible than hard knee—try this setting on a lead vocal or lyrical instrument for inconspicuous level control.

Hard knee dynamic control is more extreme and much less sonically forgiving. Try hard knee limiting when absolute level control is necessary.

The dynamic action matches the word picture—soft knee creates a gently rounded level adjustment; hard knee creates a sharp angle.

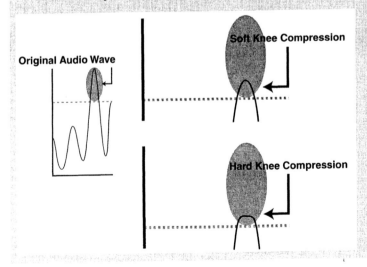

Original Audio Wave

Soft Knee Compression

Hard Knee Compression

processing control that should allow for most musical and artistic needs. Vocalists and voice-over talent with emphatic and dynamic diction often require fast attack time settings to compensate for naturally exaggerated transient. Other instruments, such as bass guitar, violin, and some synthesized sounds, might be able to take advantage of longer attack times. Fast attack time settings have the potential to make a recording sound unnaturally lifeless and weak; however, slow attack time settings might result in an overexaggerated transient. Approach each situation with musical, emotional, and artistic considerations.

Audio Example 3
Fast and Slow Attack Times Compared

Listen to this comparison of the effect of fast and slow attack times during compression.

Release

The release time setting determines how long it takes the amplifying circuitry to turn the level back up to its original level once the signal no longer exceeds the threshold. Release times between 0.5 and 1.5 seconds typically produce desirable results. When using extreme compression or limiting, the release time setting is very important. If the setting is too slow, the amplifying circuitry will never get the chance to turn back up to its original level, even once the signal ceases to exceed the threshold. If the setting is too fast, the amplifying circuitry will constantly and rapidly lower and raise the signal level as it moves above and below the threshold. This can produce an annoying and obviously processed sound.

Hard Knee/Soft Knee

Hard knee/soft knee selection determines how the compressor reacts to the signal once it passes this threshold and the amplifier circuitry engages. Whereas,

Metering Dynamic Control:
VU Meter versus LEDs versus On-screen

Each dynamic processor provides a method to measure the amount of gain reduction occurring at any given time. Whereas, a typical meter reads from left to right to indicate the amount of signal present, a compressor/limiter meter typically moves from right to left to indicate the amount of signal decrease.

When a traditional VU meter indicates gain reduction, there is no level change as long as the meter is resting at the far right side. As the level is decreased, the meter moves to the left—the numbers on the meter represent decibels of gain reduction.

When a series of LEDs are used to indicate gain reduction, each LED that illuminates indicates more gain reduction. The numbers under each LED show the amount of gain reduction.

Computer-based compressor/limiters use an on-screen graphic representation of either of these metering systems.

Both meters indicate 7 dB of gain reduction.

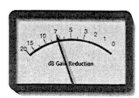
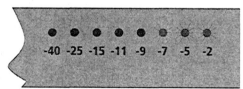

Side Chain Control of the Level-Changing Circuitry

Use the side chain send and return to control dynamics from an external source. This illustration demonstrates a common use for side chain inserts during compression or limiting.

Notice the compressor inputs and outputs are connected in the normal manner—the actual audio signal does not pass through the equalizer. The side chain send routes the audio to the equalizer, then the signal is equalized to accentuate a problem frequency.

Once it has been equalized, the signal is patched back into the unit through the side chain return. When the side chain circuit is enabled, the level detection circuit reacts to the equalized signal instead of the normal input.

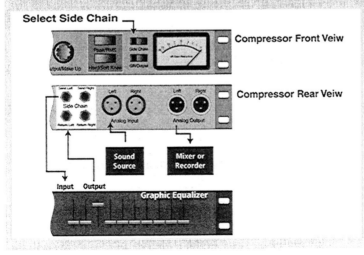

the ratio control determines the severity of compression, the knee determines how severely and immediately the compressor acts on that signal.

When the compressor is set on soft knee and the signal exceeds the threshold, the amplitude is gradually reduced throughout the first 5 dB, or so, of gain reduction. When the compressor is set on hard knee and the signal exceeds the threshold, it is rapidly and severely reduced in amplitude. The hard knee/soft knee settings are still dependent on the ratio, attack, release, and threshold settings. The knee setting specifically relates to how the amplifier circuitry reacts at the onset of compression or limiting.

The difference between hard knee and soft knee compression is more apparent at extreme compression ratios and gain reduction. Soft knee compression is most useful during high-ratio compression or limiting. The gentle approach of the soft knee setting is least obvious as the compressor begins gain reduction. Hard knee settings are very efficient when extreme and immediate limiting is called for, especially when used on audio containing an abundance of transient peaks.

Peak/RMS (Detection)

RMS refers to average signal amplitude based on the mathematical function of the Root Mean Square. Peak refers to immediate and transient amplitude levels, which occur frequently throughout most audio recordings. The Peak/RMS setting determines whether the compressor/limiter responds to average amplitude changes or peak amplitude changes. RMS compression is more gentle and unobtrusive than peak compression. Peak compression is well suited to limiting applications. It responds quickly and efficiently to incoming amplitude changes containing transient information.

Metering Gain Reduction

Compressor/limiters provide various means to gauge the amount of gain reduction. Some use a series of LEDs, which illuminate from right to left when the amplifying circuitry is reducing gain. When no LEDs are illuminated, there is no gain reduction. Once reduction begins, each LED is labelled to indicate the amount of signal decrease (in decibels).

Another common metering system utilizes a standard VU meter, operating in reverse. When the pin is all the way to the right (the normal, at rest, position), there's no gain reduction. As the level is decreased, the meter moves from right to left, indicating gain reduction in decibels as labelled on the meter face. This system often utilizes the VU meter in a double capacity—a switch toggles the status from audio level to gain reduction.

Side Chain

The side chain provides an avenue for activating the level-control circuitry from a source other than the audio signal running the unit.

Any audio source can be patched into the Side Chain input for creative applications. However, it's common to run a split from the audio signal through an equalizer then back into the side chain. In this way, the equalizer can be boosted at a specific frequency and cut at others, allowing the user to select a problem frequency to trigger gain reduction. This technique works very well when low frequency pops or thumps must be compressed while the rest of the audio signal is left unaffected, or when certain high-frequency transients must be controlled.

Listen to the following audio examples highlighting the sonic impact of different compressor/limiter settings. The acoustic guitar is often compressed and in these examples it provides an excellent comparison. With its clean, clear sound and transient attack, the parameter adjustments are very apparent.

Audio Example 4
Acoustic Guitar – No Compression

This acoustic guitar, recorded without compression, has clean sound, however, it has a wide dynamic range. Notice the difference between the level of the loudest sound and the softest sound.

Audio Example 5
Acoustic Guitar – Variations in Attack Time

Notice the change in the attack of each note. By increasing and decreasing the attack time, intimacy and sonic impact change dramatically.

Audio Example 6
Acoustic Guitar—Long and Short Release Times

With the release time set too short, the processor is continually active, risking sonic degradation. With the release time set too short, the level changes become very noticeable.

Sound Advice on Dynamic Processors

Acoustic Guitar—Ratios From Compression to Limiting

Each ratio setting provides a different result, from gentle gain control to the brick wall.

Acoustic Guitar—Adjusting the Threshold For Optimum Sonics

Listen to the changing sound as the threshold moves down into the signal amplitude. If the threshold is too high, there is no dynamic compression. If the threshold includes too much of the amplitude, the level-changing circuitry (VCA, DCA, Optical Am, etc.) is always working; this typically produces a thin, weak, or strained sound.

Acoustic Guitar—Adjusting the Knee and Peak/RMS Settings

With the ratio set at 7:1, attack time at 10 ms, release time at .5 seconds, and the threshold set for 6 dB of gain reduction, notice the sonic difference as I switch from soft to hard knee, and from Peak to RMS detection.

Should I Use the Compressor/Limiter On Input or Output?

The compressor/limiter is typically used on input; however, there are valid applications for this tool at each stage of the signal path. Compression and limiting provide an efficient means of controlling the level that's recorded to tape, hard disk, or any other analog or digital media. Recording instruments with a wide dynamic range often requires constant level adjustments to insure a consistently acceptable signal-to-noise ratio. These level changes can be performed manually, although they're typically much more reliable when performed electronically.

It is common to compress or re-compress audio tracks or groups during mixdown. Compressing the lead vocal or a stereo group of backing vocals during mixdown provides the engineer the opportunity to finely craft their positioning within the dynamic audio spectrum.

However, avoid over-compressing any signal. Part of the power of audio rests in its dynamic content. When robbed of dynamic contrast, music and other audio sources lose impact. A mix devoid of dynamic contrast is tedious for the listener. Music is, at its very essence, a balance of tension and release. Sound that remains constant in amplitude and energy provides no release and eventually wears the listener out. Strive to find the best dynamic contrast for your music.

Setup Suggestions For Compressor/Limiter

- Adjust Ratio to determine function. Settings below 10:1 produce compression; settings 10:1 to infinity:1 produce limiting.

- Set attack time fast or slow, depending on the audio source and desired effect

- Set release time to about .5 seconds for general use.

- Select Soft Knee for gentle compression, or Hard Knee for limiting applications

- Select RMS for most compression applications, or Peak for most limiting applications.

- Adjust the threshold for the desired amount of gain reduction.

- Consider all rules carefully, then break them at will, and intentionally, any time the music demands.

How Much Is Enough?

Though the musical and artistic needs of any recording must dictate the use and application of all available tools, there are some guidelines for most tasks which should be considered.

Compression and limiting are generally most effective when gain reduction occurs several times throughout a recording, yet most of the audio is left untouched—beneath the threshold. If the compressor/limiter is always turning the signal down and back up again, optimum gain reduction is not being achieved; in addition, adverse side effects called pumping and breathing occur.

Pumping

Pumping is the result of the level-control circuitry reducing gain, as the amplitude exceeds the threshold, then turning it back up again as the signal dips below the threshold. In some very "in-your-face" commercial pop music, a certain degree of pumping is acceptable to some artists; however, there are other ways to keep the mix optimally present without risking serious audio quality degradation. Pumping is often viewed as more extreme than breathing.

Breathing

Breathing is like pumping, although the actual breathing sounds are derived from a signal with a high noise content. As the noise, or room ambience, is decreased and increased as it crosses the threshold, it creates a sound similar to breathing. Whereas pumping and breathing are essentially the same technical anomaly, pumping is often associated with a full range signal, and breathing is associated with an airy, high-frequency sound.

Audio Example 10
Pumping and Breathing Examples

Listen to these examples of pumping and breathing. Notice the difference in the effect as the audio content changes.

Commercial Pop Music

Commercial pop music is often highly compressed and limited. The fact that most highly commercial music is heard in listening environments with intrusive ambience motivates artists and producers to contain their recording to a very narrow dynamic range—the music must be heard over road noise, crowd noise, clanking glasses, breaking plates, and the "blue-light special" announcement. Most commercial recordings head immediately up to 0VU and stay there through the duration of the song; this doesn't make for a very emotionally dynamic work of art, but it does produce music that consistently holds the listener's attention.

Classical Recording

Classical recordists typically use compression and limiting sparingly. The dynamic realism of a symphony or soloist—held in high regard throughout the classical listening community—is very integral to artistic expression. Too much dynamic processing changes the balance between ambience and music, altering the individualism of a highly-skilled ensemble or artist.

When included, dynamic processing is typically very subtle and understated. Limiting is sometimes used for extreme peaks, or gentle compression might be included to help smooth out the loudest sections; however, dynamic processing is almost always subtle and sonically inconspicuous.

The Purist and Compression

The audio purist always strives to eliminate amplifying circuitry from the signal path. Therefore, many engineers prefer to control levels manually, using a mixer fader, to facilitate the most accurate, pristine, and natural-sounding recording. However, compressors and limiters have been so commonly used in commercial music recording that the sound achieved by their use has become expected; the impact, dynamic control, and punch that they provide has become, in some producer/ engineers' opinions, sonically essential.

Multiband Compressor/Limiters

Dynamic processing of a full-bandwidth signal presents a unique set of considerations. A single instrument or voice is typically functional in a specific frequency range; extreme bandwidth isn't a real consideration. In these instances, a full-bandwidth compressor/limiter is effective and preferred. On the other hand, a full-bandwidth recording (like a complete mix of commercial pop song) contains an impressive amount of all frequencies. Low-frequency content contains the greatest amplitude, so, when running this type of signal through a full-range compressor/limiter, the low frequencies tend to activate the gain reduction circuitry first and most often. As the mix level changes in response to the bass frequencies, the high frequencies also change; they decrease during gain reduction, then they increase as the signal is turned back up.

Multiband Compression

This compression software contains three separate sets of compression parameters. Each set of parameters controls only the frequency band corresponding to its specific selection. This tool provides excellent capabilities for exact placement of a sound within almost any dynamic and tonal context.

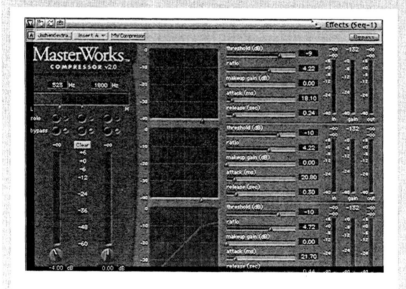

Full-range Recording Through a Normal
Compressor

*Listen to this example of a full-range recording
passing through a normal compressor/limiter.
Notice how the high frequencies ride along with the
lows, as gain reduction comes and goes.*

A multiband compressor/limiter
divides the audio into multiple frequency
ranges (frequency bands). Each frequency
band is compressed separately. Whereas
the audible spectrum is typically divided
into lows, mids, and highs, the actual
crossover points, between bands, is often
user-adjustable. Since each frequency range
is dynamically controlled independent of
the others, there is less audible pumping
and breathing, and the mix stays more
consistently in the forefront of the dynamic
spectrum.

Most commercial mixes pass through
some form of multiband compression,

eventually. Mastering engineers use these tools to help raise the overall level and impact of recordings so they'll sound loud and full in comparison with other professional recordings. Overuse of the multiband compressor can result in a lifeless sound. On the other hand, tastefully aggressive multiband dynamic control can result in a very punchy and impressive recording.

Be aware that as the bands compress separately, the mix changes slightly: when the low-frequency gain is reduced, the highs and mids will probably stick out more in the mix; or, when the mids are reduced the vocals might be suddenly buried. Careful selection of ratios and crossover points between bands will usually solve these problems, though these details do require your utmost attention.

Full-range Recording Through a Multiband
Compressor

Listen to this example of a full-bandwidth mix passing through a multiband compressor/limiter. Notice the change in sound as the processor switches in and out.

De-essers

A de-esser is a frequency specific compressor that reacts quickly to signals with strong high-frequency content—in particular, the common frequency range of the letters "s," "t," and "k." The purpose of the de-esser is to compensate for poorly compressed vocals. When a vocal track is recorded with the threshold too low and the attack time too slow, the initial transient sounds are overexaggerated, resulting in over-modulation of analog tape, over-stimulation of reverberation, and just a generally obnoxiously sibilant sound. Since the de-esser reacts quickly to high frequencies, it can usually solve a sibilance problem.

Most compressor/limiters can function as a de-esser. Simply select a fast attack time, patch the side chain to an external equalizer which has the frequencies between about 3 and 6 kHz boosted (depending on the sound being de-essed), select the side chain as the processor trigger, then adjust the threshold so gain reduction occurs whenever a transient problem occurs.

Tube versus Solid-state Compressor/Limiters

Compressor/limiters, throughout the years, have been manufactured using vacuum tube circuitry, solid-state circuitry, and even a combination of both. Some engineers just love old equipment: they love the look; they love the history; they love the feel; and they love the sound. Realistically, high-quality compressors and limiters are very useful, whether they use tube or solid-state technology. Listen to the tool, then choose the sound that provides the best support for the musical vision.

Sound Advice on Dynamic Processors

Tube technology typically sounds warmer and fuller than solid-state technology, especially as it's pushed to the limit of its capability. When a vacuum-tube audio circuit reaches distortion the waveform is smoother and more rounded than a comparable solid-state waveform. In comparison, distortion of a solid-state circuit causes the waveform to be clipped off in an extreme way, creating a harsh and brittle sound. For this reason, musical styles that contain a wide dynamic range, or very aggressive instrumentation and orchestration, are often recorded using tube technology.

Solid-state technology is, in theory, far quieter than tube technology. Utilizing high-quality solid-state compressor/limiters is very desirable in a context where the amplifying circuitry is not being over taxed. They can be the most accurate and sonically purer compressors and limiters, as long as the processor has plenty of headroom to avoid any kind of waveform distortion.

Sonic Comparison of Tube and Solid-State Compression

Gate/Expander

The gate and expander are in the same family as the compressor/limiter. They're also dependent on a VCA. In addition, the VCA still turns the signal down. When the VCA is all the way up, the signal is at the same level as if the VCA weren't in the circuit.

When the compressor/limiter senses the signal passing the threshold in an upward way, it turns down the signal that's above the threshold. The amount of gain reduction is determined by the ratio control. In contrast, when the gate/expander senses the signal passing the threshold in a downward way, the VCA turns the signal down even further. In other words, everything that's below the threshold is turned down.

Sound Advice on Dynamic Processors

What are the controls on a gate/expander? The controls on the gate/expander are essentially the same as the controls on a compressor/limiter. The threshold is the control that determines how much of the signal is acted on by the unit. The attack and release times do the same thing here that they did on the compressor: They control how quickly the unit acts once the signal has passed the threshold and how fast the unit turns the signal back up once the signal is no longer below the threshold.

The range control on the expander/gate correlates to the ratio control on the compressor/limiter. In fact, some multifunction dynamic processors use the same knob to control both ratio and range. The ratio on a compressor determines how far the VCA turns the signal down once it passes the threshold in an upward direction. The range on a gate/expander determines how far down the VCA will turn the signal once it passes the threshold in a downward direction.

When the signal gets below the threshold and the range setting tells the VCA to turn all the way off, the unit is called a gate. When the signal is below the threshold, the gate is closed. The gate closes behind the sound and doesn't open again until the signal is above the threshold.

The range can also be adjusted so that the VCA only turns down the signal part of the way once it gets below the threshold. In this case, the unit is called an expander.

A gate is called a gate because it opens and closes when it senses the signal come and go across the threshold.

An expander is called an expander because it expands the dynamic range of the music. It creates a bigger difference between the softer and the louder sound by turning the softer parts down.

Sound Advice on Dynamic Processors

The most common type of expander doesn't turn the louder parts up; it just seems to in relation to the softer parts. Specifically, an expander that turns the softer sounds down is called a downward expander. There is also an upward expander which turns the louder part up even louder. Upward expanders aren't very common and are somewhat noisy and difficult to control in a medium such as magnetic tape. Unless I specify otherwise, I'll refer to a downward expander throughout this series simply as an expander.

The following audio examples demonstrate the practical benefit of these important tools. Listen to each example then envision how to apply the techniques to your unique situation.

Anything above the threshold is not affected by the gate/expander's VCA. The gate/expander turns anything below the threshold down or off.

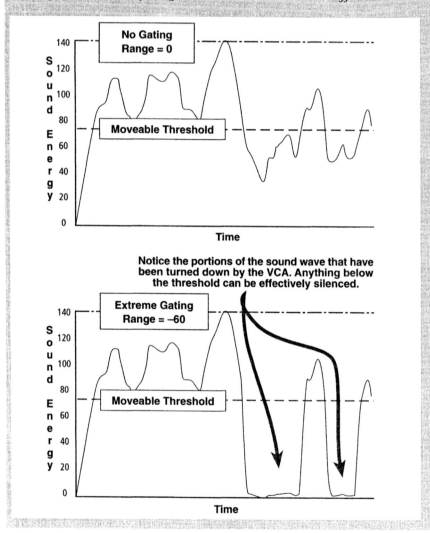

No Gating
Range = 0

Moveable Threshold

Time

Notice the portions of the sound wave that have been turned down by the VCA. Anything below the threshold can be effectively silenced.

Extreme Gating
Range = −60

Moveable Threshold

Time

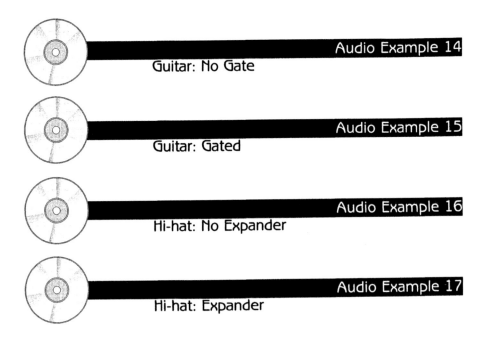

Audio Example 14
Guitar: No Gate

Audio Example 15
Guitar: Gated

Audio Example 16
Hi-hat: No Expander

Audio Example 17
Hi-hat: Expander

These dynamic range processors are all very useful, and often essential, in creating professional sounds. Each unit offers many creative and musical possibilities. As we study the individual instruments and their unique sound schemes, we'll use these processors over and over.

Dynamic Processing Guitar

It's very common to use a compressor on an electric guitar. Most guitars have a very wide dynamic range, and many instruments have uneven string volumes due to substandard adjustment of the pickups and string height. A compressor is what gives a guitar that smooth always-in-your-face sound. It puts all the notes and chords into a very narrow dynamic range so there might not be much (if any) volume difference between a single note and a full chord.

An outboard compressor designed for studio use can do a good job on guitar, but it's normal for the boxes made especially for guitar to work most conveniently in a player's setup. Most guitarists use a compressor in their setup, so when recording their guitar sounds, you usually don't need to compress much, if at all. When the guitarist has his stuff together, your job as the recordist is pretty simple. Whether you're running direct in or miking the speaker cabinet, your job is to capture the existing sound accurately rather than creating and shaping a new sound. You can put a compressor on the signal that's coming into the mixer if you need to, but ideally, the guitarist will have a properly adjusted compressor in his kit.

In a guitar setup that uses several effects, the compressor should be the first effect in the chain. This will give the best sounding results and will help guard the rest of the effects from strong signals that might overdrive their inputs.

A compressor can efficiently even out the volume of different notes. This usually makes the guitarist's job easier. With a healthy amount of compression, the guitar will sustain longer, plus each note will be audible (even if the guitarist has sloppy technique). Listen to the difference the compressor makes on the simple guitar sounds in the following audio examples.

Audio Example 18

No Compression

This audio example was performed and recorded with no compression.

Audio Example 19

With Compression

This example demonstrates the same part as the previous example with a healthy amount of compression. I've used a ratio of 4:1 with about 10 dB of gain reduction.

Dynamic Processing Bass

Compressing the Bass

Bass is usually compressed. There's a big difference in level between notes on many basses. Some notes read very hot on the VU meter and some read very cold. Since the compressor automatically turns down the signal above the user set threshold, it helps keep the stronger notes under control.

If the bass notes are evened out in volume by the compressor, the bass track stays more constant in the mix and supplies a solid foundation for the song. If the bass is left uncompressed, the bass part can tend to sound especially loud and boomy on certain notes and disappear altogether on others. More consistent levels from note to note typically provide the best foundation for most recordings.

A compressor becomes especially useful if a player snaps a high note or thumps a low note because the level changes can be extreme. Not only does the compressor help control the louder bass sounds but it also helps the subtleties come through more clearly. If the loud sounds are turned down, the entire track can be boosted to achieve a proper VU reading. As the track is turned up, the softer sounds are turned up, which makes them more audible in the mix.

Non-Compressed Bass

The bass performance in this example is not compressed. Notice the difference between the loudest and softest sounds.

Compressed Bass

This time the bass is compressed with a ratio of 4:1 and gain reduction of up to 6dB. This example peaks at the same level as the previous example, but notice how much more even the notes sound.

If the bass part is very consistent in level and the player has a good, solid predictable touch, you might not even need compression. I've been able to get some great bass sounds without compression. This only happens when you have a great player with predictable and disciplined technique, a great instrument and the appropriate bass part. Aside from these factors, most bass parts need compression.

If the bass part includes snaps and thumps, consider limiting. With a limiter, most of the notes are left unaffected, but the snaps and thumps are limited. Limiting is the same as compression, but with a ratio above 10:1.

If the limiter is set correctly, the bass part can be totally unprocessed on everything but a strong thump. The thump might exceed the threshold by 10dB, but if the ratio is 10:1 or higher, the output of the compressor won't show more than a 1 dB increase.

Follow this procedure to correctly adjust the limiter:

1. Set the ratio control to about 10:1.

2. Set the attack time to fast.

3. Adjust the threshold so that gain reduction only registers on the snaps and thumps.

Audio Example 22

Snaps Not Limited

This bass part isn't limited. Notice how much louder the snaps are than the rest of the notes. Also, note that the normal level is low in order to keep the snaps from oversaturating the tape.

Audio Example 23

Limited Snaps

Once the bass part is limited the snaps aren't much louder than the rest of the notes, and the entire part sounds louder because the limiter has turned down the peaks.

Dynamic Processing Drums

Gating the Snare

As we discovered with the kick drum track, it can be helpful to gate the snare track on playback from the multitrack. The gate will eliminate any channel crosstalk from the drum machine or multitrack and, more importantly, it'll eliminate tape noise between the snare hits.

Gate the Snare

On this snare track I boost the high frequencies to accentuate the snare sound; however, turning the highs up also turns the tape noise up. Listen as the snare plays. After a few seconds, I insert the gate. Notice the change in noise level between hits. This technique also works well to eliminate leakage when recording live drums.

Compressing the Snare Sound

A common technique on snare drum that's also very popular on toms and kick is compression. Compression has two primary effects on drum tracks. First, since the compressor is an automatic level control, it evens out the volume of each hit. This can be a very good thing on a commercial rock tune, where the snare part is a simple backbeat on two and four. The compressor keeps the level even so that a weak hit doesn't detract from the groove.

Gating

Set the gate threshold just above the noise to keep the drum sound but to eliminate the unwanted noise. Everything below the threshold will be turned down or off.

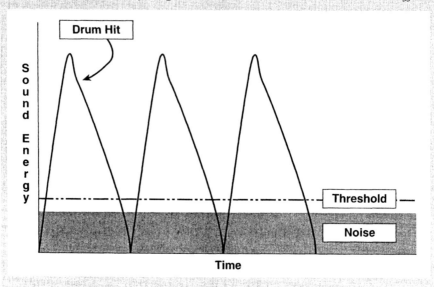

The second benefit of compression is its ability, with proper use, to accentuate the attack of the snare drum. If the compressor controls are adjusted correctly, we can exaggerate the attack of the snare, giving the snare a very aggressive and penetrating edge. This technique involves setting the attack time of the compressor slow enough so that the attack is not compressed but the remaining portion of the sound is compressed.

This is how to set the compressor to exaggerate the attack of any drum:

1. Set the ratio between 3:1 and 10:1.

2. Set the release time at about .5 seconds. This will need to be adjusted according to the length of the snare sound. Just be sure the LEDs showing gain reduction have all gone off before the next major hit of the drum. This doesn't apply to fills, but if the snare is hitting on 2 and 4, the LEDs should be out before each hit.

3. At this point, set the attack time to its fastest setting.

4. Adjust the threshold for 3 to 9 dB of gain reduction.

5. Finally, readjust the attack time. As you slow the attack time of the compressor, it doesn't react in time to compress the transient, but it can react in time to compress the rest of the drum sound.

Exaggerating the Snare Transient

This graph shows the sound energy of a snare drum without compression. Threshold and attack time are only indicated as references.

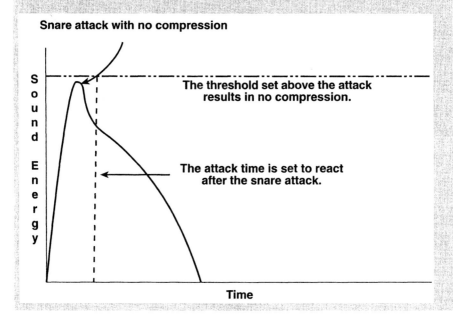

Snare attack with no compression

S o u n d   E n e r g y

The threshold set above the attack results in no compression.

The attack time is set to react after the snare attack.

Time

Sound Advice on Dynamic Processors

The Result of Compression

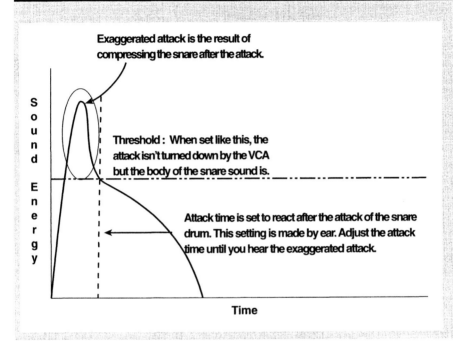

Exaggerated attack is the result of compressing the snare after the attack.

Sound Energy

Threshold : When set like this, the attack isn't turned down by the VCA but the body of the snare sound is.

Attack time is set to react after the attack of the snare drum. This setting is made by ear. Adjust the attack time until you hear the exaggerated attack.

Time

Compression isn't musically effective on some jazz styles where the snare may be doing little jabs and fills within the beat that are mostly for the feel. These jabs and fills aren't really meant to be heard predominantly in the mix, so the compressor might ruin the feel of a jazz drum track rather than solidifying or enhancing the feel.

Listen to the following example to hear the difference in sound when compressing a snare drum.

Audio Example 25
No Compression

Audio Example 26
Compressed Snare

This example uses the same snare drum from the previous example. This time a compressor, adjusted to emphasize the attack, is in the signal path.

Compressing drum sounds has a practical disadvantage. Since the compressor is turning down the loudest hits, the entire track can be turned up, which also turns up the noise (and leakage from the other drums if you're recording acoustic drums) in relation to the snare hits. This gives us another reason to gate the track on playback.

If you gate the tape track before you compress the tape track, the gate turns down the tape noise, so as the compressor turns back up, there's no more tape noise to turn up. Always place the gate before the compressor in the signal path when gating and compressing a tape track. Keep in mind that though most current digital gear is virtually noise-free, these principles (which are very valuable in the analog domain) can be used creatively in the process of producing innovative music. I'm often thankful for the techniques I've learned in each phase of my recording life and draw on them frequently. Whereas the following examples use tape noise to demonstrate the compression/gating process, the same technique could be used to isolate the tom mics from the rest of the kit, or a sax mic from the band, or even dialogue mics from street noise.

Listen to the snare in the following examples. Its dynamics are progressively controlled.

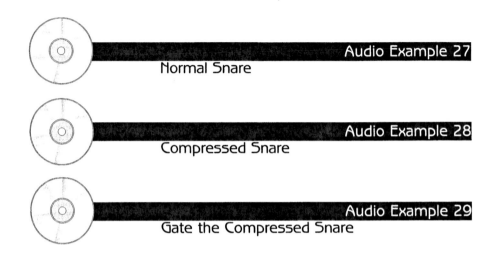

Audio Example 27
Normal Snare

Audio Example 28
Compressed Snare

Audio Example 29
Gate the Compressed Snare

Dynamic Processing Vocals

Compressor/Limiter/Gate/Expander

Vocalists almost always use a wide dynamic range during the course of a song. Often they'll sing very tenderly and quietly during one measure and then emotionally blast you with all the volume and energy they can muster up during the next. Most of the time you need a compressor/limiter to avoid overloading your recorder with signal.

As the compressor's VCA (voltage controlled amplifier) turns down the signal that passes the threshold, the entire vocal track occupies a narrower dynamic range. When the vocal is in a narrow dynamic range, the loud sounds are easier to record because they aren't out of control, plus the softer sounds can be heard and understood better in the mix.

Dynamic Range

Compression can be the single most important contributor to a vocal recording that's consistently audible and under-standable in a mix. Most lead vocals on commercial hit recordings are compressed. So far in this course, we've seen each instrument benefit from compression, and vocals realize much of the same benefit.

Some producers don't like the sound of the compressor's VCA turning up and down so they'll record the vocal tracks without compression. But during mix-down, the engineer still needs to manually ride the vocal level to compensate for the wide vocal dynamic range. The engineer in this case is acting as a manual compressor, substituting for the automatic VCA controlled compressor.

When recording vocal tracks, even with compression, the engineer often rides the record level fader to compensate for the loudest parts of the song. This method works very well if the engineer is familiar with the song and the artist's interpretation, but it also has the potential to cause more problems than it solves. Practice and experience provide the necessary skills to successfully perform this technique.

The benefit of riding the record level fader while recording vocal tracks is the need for less compression. If you can cut 5 or 6dB off the hottest part of the track by riding the fader, you've decreased the amount of leveling required by the compressor. Less action from the compressor almost always results in a clearer, more natural sound.

These graphs represent vocal energy (the curve) in relation to the rest of the mix (the gray area). The top graph (not compressed) shows the volume of some lyrics sinking into the mix, probably being covered up.

The bottom graph indicates the same performance and lyric after being compressed. This time the lyrics peak at the same level, but after being compressed notice that the softer lyrics are turned up so they can be heard above the rest of the mix. Once the compressor/limiter has decreased the dynamic range and levels have been adjusted to attain the proper peak level, your vocals should be consistently understandable. More emotional nuance will be heard and felt.

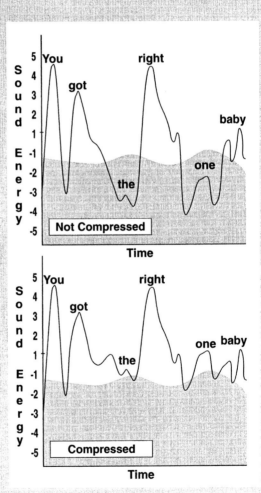

Even though the most common vocal recording technique utilizes a compressor/ limiter, your choice to include a compressor in your vocal recordings should be based on the vocalist, the song, vocal range, dynamic range, emotion and other musical considerations. Avoid ruts. Evaluate each situation separately. There are many times when a compressor is your best friend when recording vocals. There are also many situations where the compressor sucks the life out of a brilliant performance.

Compression
Vocals are usually compressed using a medium-fast attack time (3 to 5ms), a medium-long release time (from a half second to a second), and a ratio between 3:1 and 7:1 with about 6dB of gain reduction at the loudest part of the track.

A vocalist who is used to recording in the studio can make your job much easier. Less compression is needed on singers who use mic technique to compensate for their changes in level. A seasoned professional will back off a bit on the loud notes and move in a bit on the soft notes. This technique on the vocalist's part will help you record the most controlled, understandable and natural sounding vocal track. If you set the compressor so it indicates no gain reduction most of the time with 2 to 4 dB of reduction on the loudest notes, and if the vocal is always understandable and smooth sounding, that's good.

Listen to the vocal track with rhythm accompaniment in the following audio example. The vocal isn't compressed. Notice how it sometimes disappears in the mix.

Audio Example 30
Vocal Without Compression

Audio Example 31
Vocal With 4:1 Compression

This example demonstrates the same vocal, compressed using a ratio of 4:1 with up to about 6dB of gain reduction. The peak level is the same but listen for the softer notes—they're easier to hear and understand.

Sibilance

Avoid overcompressing the vocals. If the attack time isn't instantaneous or at least nearly instantaneous, it's possible to compress most of the words but not the initial sounds. For instance, a word starting with "s" or "t" might have a very fast attack—an attack too fast to be turned down by the compressor. The initial "s" or "t" will sound unnaturally loud and, like other transient sounds, won't register accurately on a VU meter. These exaggerated attacks are called sibilant sounds. When sibilant sounds are recorded too hot, your recordings will have a splatting type of distortion every time sibilance occurs. Sibilance distortion also happens when a sibilant sound occurs in the middle or end of a word.

Sibilance

These graphs represent the changes in amplitude over time of the word "Sally." The top graph has an average level of about 0 VU, but the "S" is about 3 dB above the remainder of the word "...ally."

If the compressor's attack time is slow enough that the VCA doesn't begin to act until after the "S" and if the remainder of the word is compressed, exaggeration of the initial sibilant sound results.

The bottom graph represents the result of compressing the word "Sally." Notice the difference in level between the "S" and the remainder of the word. This type of compression technique, when used in moderation (1 to 3 dB), can help increase intelligibility and understandability. However, this scenario can lead to overexaggerated sibilance risking unnecessary analog distortion, digital clipping, and hyper-excited reverberation effects.

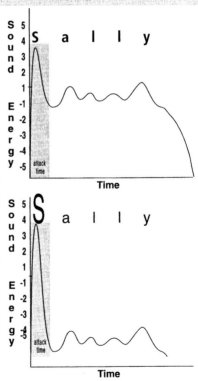

Each singer has a unique sibilant character. Bone structure, physical alignment of the vocalist's teeth, jaw position and size all play a part in exactly how they produce sibilant sounds. Some vocalists don't produce strong transients; other vocalists produce mega transients. I find that a singer with straight teeth and a perfect bite typically produces a very strong transient on consonants that have a "hiss" sound ("s," "t," "ch," "zh," "sh").

Sibilance problems often slide by when recording to the multitrack (analog or digital), but when cassettes are duplicated you might find a big problem with sibilance distortion. Small tape has less headroom and therefore distorts easier than most multitrack recorders.

Sound Advice on Dynamic Processors

The De-esser

Use a de-esser to help compensate for sibilance problems. A de-esser is a fast acting compressor set to turn down the high frequencies that are present in the sibilant sounds and is often built into a compressor/limiter. If the de-esser is activated, the VCA responds to the highs instead of all frequencies at once, therefore turning down the exaggerated sibilance. De-essers often have a control that sweeps a range of high frequencies, letting the user choose which high frequency will be compressed. The threshold control lets you set the de-esser so it only turns down the high frequencies of the sibilant sounds but leaves the rest of the track alone.

Good compression technique, proper mic choice and positioning are usually the answer to sibilance problems. But these problems have become particularly problematic with the growth of digital recording. Digital metering helps you record the full range of the transient accurately so any transfer to analog media, such as cassette tape, provide opportunity for sibilance distortion. Through education and the proper use of compression and de-essing you can record vocal tracks that are clean and clear and work well within any musical structure.

Summary

Compressor/limiters are an integral part of most recordings. Proper and wise use of the control they offer can help create a finely crafted and sonically controlled musical work. Improper or careless use of these tools can minimize the artistic and dynamic impact you work so hard to achieve.

Start practicing! Keep your eye open for good bargains on vintage—or soon to be vintage—gear. Some of the gear I used and rejected 20 years ago has become kind of trendy these days. Anyway you look at it, these are tools to help create music. One unit might be terrible for one application and brilliant for another. Keep an open mind and above all, use your ears—not popular opinion—to determine the perfect tool for the job.